# Sophie W
## about Confirmation

Debby Bradley

Illustrated by
Lula Guzmán

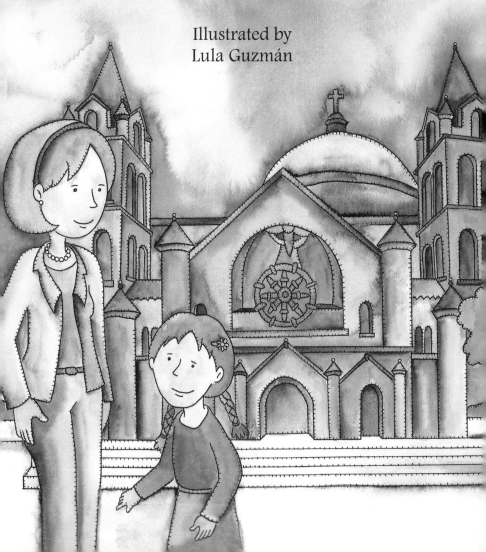

## Dedication

Grateful
for love and support from my husband, Bill,
and children Claire Marie, Teman John Kaiser,
and Molly Renee.

Blessed
to have as my first religious examples
Fr. Bill Vos and Ade Ledermann.

Thankful
to have witnessed the inspiration of these who have
joined the communion of saints: Kenneth Besetzny,
Judith Batton, Helen Marais, and John Kaiser.

Imprimi Potest:
Harry Grile, CSsR, Provincial
Denver Province, The Redemptorists

Published by Liguori Publications
Liguori, Missouri 63057

To order, call 800-325-9521
www.liguori.org

p ISBN: 978-0-7648-2349-7
e ISBN: 978-0-7648-6884-9

Liguori Publications, a nonprofit corporation, is an apostolate of The Redemptorists. To learn more about The Redemptorists, visit Redemptorists.com.

Printed in the United States of America
18 17 16 15 14  /  5 4 3 2 1
First Edition

There once was a little girl.

Her name was Sophie.

Sophie wondered about many things.

Today Sophie wondered about a celebration for her cousin Frederic.

"Why are we going to a different church
for Frederic today?" she asked.

Mommy said, "Frederic and his classmates
are being confirmed at the cathedral."

"What does that mean?" Sophie asked.

Mommy said, "*Confirmation* is a sacrament.
A sacrament is a special celebration that reminds
us that God wants to be present in our lives.

"We celebrate these times
with other Christians.

"Do you remember when we talked about baptism, Eucharist, and reconciliation?"

Sophie's face lit up. "I remember those!"

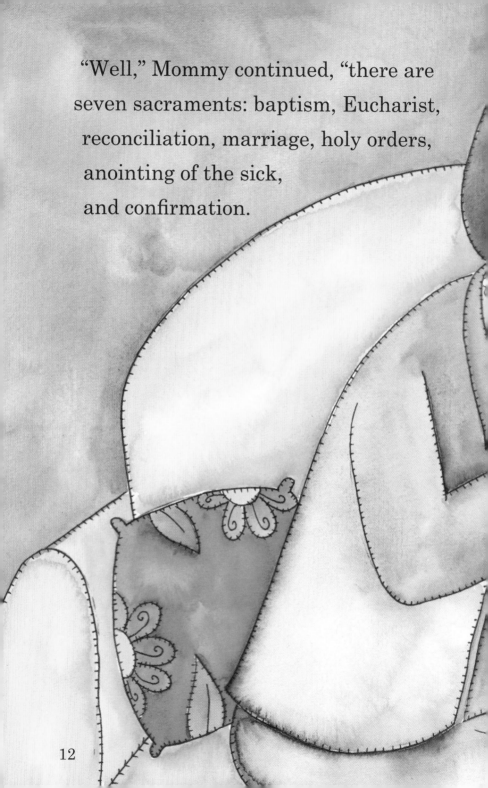

"Well," Mommy continued, "there are seven sacraments: baptism, Eucharist, reconciliation, marriage, holy orders, anointing of the sick, and confirmation.

"The first sacrament Frederic
received was baptism."

"That's when he became a member of the Christian family, right?" Sophie asked.

"That's right. Next, he made his first reconciliation and then his first Eucharist."

Sophie exclaimed,
"That's when Frederic
received Jesus in a
special way at Mass!"

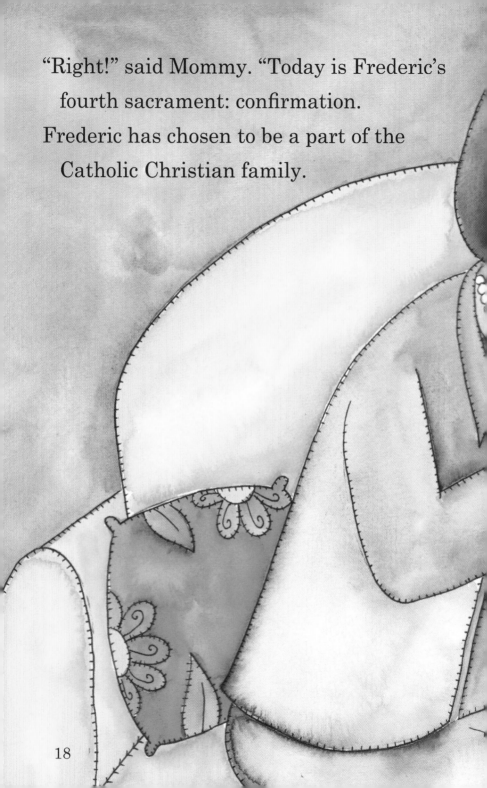

"Right!" said Mommy. "Today is Frederic's fourth sacrament: confirmation. Frederic has chosen to be a part of the Catholic Christian family.

"At confirmation, Frederic receives special thinking and feeling gifts from the Holy Spirit to help him live more like Jesus.

"To get ready, he went to special classes to learn about God and our Church.

"Now we expect him to live his best like Jesus and even help others learn about God."

"I'm glad I'm not getting confirmed today," Sophie said.

"Why is that?" asked Mommy.

"Because I don't know how to go
to a class yet!"

Mommy laughed and hugged
her precious Sophie.

# Sophie Wonders
## About the Sacraments

***Sophie Wonders About Anointing***
Paperback 823411 • eBook 868672

***Sophie Wonders About Baptism***
Paperback 823473 • eBook 868856

***Sophie Wonders About Confirmation***
Paperback 823497 • eBook 868849

***Sophie Wonders About Eucharist***
Paperback 823398 • eBook 868689

***Sophie Wonders About Holy Orders***
Paperback 823435 • eBook 868658

***Sophie Wonders About Marriage***
Paperback 823510 • eBook 868863

***Sophie Wonders About Reconciliation***
Paperback 823459 • eBook 868665

To order, visit Liguori.org
or call 800-325-9521